Landforms

Islands

Cassie Mayer

Heinemann Library
Chicago, Illinois

Photo research by Heather Mauldin and Tracy Cummins
Designed by Jo Hinton-Malivoire
Printed and bound in China by South China Printing Company
11 10 09 08 07
10 9 8 7 6 5 4 3 2

Library of Congress Cataloging-in-Publication Data
Mayer, Cassie.
  Islands / Cassie Mayer.
    p. cm. — (Landforms)
  Includes bibliographical references and index.
  ISBN 1-4034-8437-6 (hc) — ISBN 1-4034-8443-0 (pb)
  ISBN 978-1-4034-8437-6 (hc) — ISBN 978-1-4034-8443-7 (pb)
  1. Islands—Juvenile literature. I. Title. II. Series.
  GB471.M192 2007
  551.42—dc22
                                    2006004673
Acknowledgments
The author and publisher are grateful to the following for permission to reproduce copyright material:
Corbis pp. **4** (river, Pat O'Hara; mountain, Royalty Free; volcano, Galen Rowell; cave, Layne Kennedy), **5** (George Steinmetz), **9** (Yann Arthus-Bertrand), **10** (Richard Hamilton Smith), **11** (Jonathan Blair), **12** (Craig Tuttle), **13** (Bob Krist), **14** (Skyscan), **21** (Chris Lisle); Getty Images **7** (Haas), **8** (Herbert), **15** (Chesley), **16** (Josef Beck), **17** (John Lawrence), **18** (Art Wolfe), **19** (Suzanne & Nick Geary), **20** (Stewart Cohen), **23** (lighthouse, Lawrence; Bay of Plenty, Chesley).

Cover photograph of the island Culebra, Puerto Rico, reproduced with permission of Corbis/Danny Lehman. Backcover image of British Virgin Islands reproduced with permission of Getty Images/Herbert.

Every effort has been made to contact copyright holders of any material reproduced in this book.
Any omissions will be rectified in subsequent printings if notice is given to the publisher.

Contents

Landforms

The land is made of different shapes.
These shapes are called landforms.

island

An island is a landform.
An island is not living.

What Is an Island?

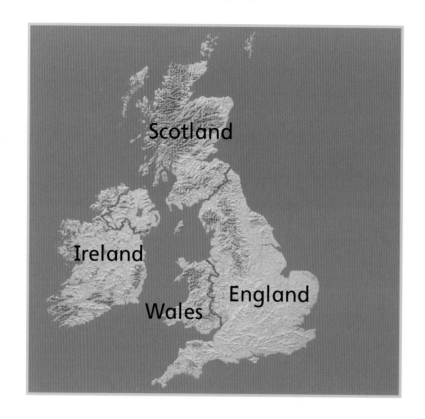

An island is land with water on all sides. Some islands are very big.

Some islands are very small.

Islands are in seas and oceans.

Islands are in rivers and lakes.

Some islands are close to each other.

A group of islands is called a chain.

Types of Islands

Some islands have warm weather.

Some islands have cold weather.

Some islands are the top of a mountain.
The mountain sticks out of the water.

Some islands are the top of a volcano.
The volcano sticks out of the water.

Features of an Island

Some islands have beaches.

Some islands have cliffs.

What Lives on an Island?

iguana

Islands are home to living things.
Plants and animals live on islands.

People live on islands, too.

Visiting Islands

People like to visit islands.

Islands show us the beauty of land and water.

Island Facts

Greenland is the largest island in the world. Most of the island is covered in ice.

Hawaii is a state. It is a group of islands. It is part of the United States.

Picture Glossary

cliff rock that is very high and steep

volcano a mountain with a hole on top

Index

Note to Parents and Teachers
This series introduces children to the concept of landforms as features that make up the earth's surface. Discuss with children landforms they are already familiar with, pointing out different landforms that exist in the area in which they live.

In this book, children explore the characteristics of islands. The photographs draw children in to the natural beauty of islands and support the concepts presented in the text. The text has been chosen with the advice of a literacy expert to enable beginning readers success reading independently or with moderate support. An expert in the field of geology was consulted to ensure accurate content. You can support children's nonfiction literacy skills by helping them use the table of contents, headings, picture glossary, and index.